Praise for *Gone To Gold Mountain*

"In *Gone To Gold Mountain*, poet Peter Ludwin brings to life the little-known story of Chea Po and his fellow Chinese gold miners, massacred in 1887 by Eastern Oregon pioneers. Ludwin embodies Chea Po and his experiences of breathtaking racism, homesickness, and dislocation. He imbues these persona poems, letters, and laments with the finely-drawn landscapes of Hells Canyon and China, glowing lanterns, and an eagle circling the canyon rim. Chea Po seems to have haunted Ludwin until finally, here, his life and death are told justly. We are the richer for it."
—Kathleen Flenniken, author of *Plume* and *Famous*

"Ludwin's haunting poems resurrect an era of vehement anti-Chinese sentiment in the U.S. by focusing on the Hells Canyon massacre in 1887—a segment of U.S. history conveniently omitted from the textbooks. To a great extent, the work's strength lies in its understated eloquence, riveting imagery, and frequent use of persona poems in different voices. With great insight, skill and compassion, Ludwin has produced a fine collection that succeeds in fleshing out this nightmare episode from our past."
—Diana Anhalt, author of *because there is no return*

GONE TO GOLD MOUNTAIN

GONE TO GOLD MOUNTAIN

poems by
Peter Ludwin

MoonPathPress

Copyright © 2016 Peter Ludwin

Poetry
ISBN 978-1-936657-24-7

Front cover photo and author photo: Lisa Schmidt
Back cover photo: Peter Ludwin
Both the front and back cover photos were taken in 2012 during a weekend conference in Lewiston, Idaho on the Chinese in Hells Canyon and the surrounding region in the 19th century. Lisa's front cover photo shows a bend in the Snake River and Hells Canyon. Peter's photo of swallowtail butterflies on a sandy bank of the Snake was taken at Chinese Massacre Cove, 65 miles up the river from Lewiston. Lisa's photo of Peter was taken in her backyard.

Design by Tonya Namura
using Minion Pro.

MoonPath Press is dedicated to publishing the finest poets of the U.S. Pacific Northwest.

MoonPath Press
PO Box 445
Tillamook, OR 97141

MoonPathPress@gmail.com

http://MoonPathPress.com

Gone to Gold Mountain

Swallows and magpies, flying in glee:
Greetings for New Year.
Daddy has gone to Gold Mountain
To earn money.
He will earn gold and silver,
Ten thousand taels.
>   —from a 19th century Cantonese nursery rhyme

Acknowledgments

Grateful acknowledgment is made to the editors of the following journals in which these poems first appeared:

Atlanta Review: "Wong Lee Talks Idaho History to a Friend"

The Comstock Review: "Trial of Compassion, Baker City, Oregon" (Special Merit Recognition recipient in the 2011 Muriel Craft Bailey Memorial Awards Contest)

Floating Bridge Review: "Meditation on a Chinese Miner"; "Chea Po to Himself at Daybreak"

Hawai'i Pacific Review: "Chea Po Addresses the Birds Shortly before His Murder by Outlaws"

The Hurricane Review: "Chea Po Remonstrates Ah Yow at Their Gold Mining Camp"; "Chea Po's Lament"; "Blue Evans, Fugitive, 1888"; "James Brewrink's Discovery in Hells Canyon"; "The Old Chinese Cemetery, Lewiston, Idaho"; "The Door Unhinged"

The Main Street Rag: "Clerk to an Investigative Reporter, Wallowa County, Oregon"

The Meadow: "Chea Po in Lewiston, Idaho, 1883"

The Mochila Review: "American Dream"; "Prospect Park"; "Chinese Remembering Ceremony, 2011"

Off the Coast: "A Chinese Woman Writes Her Beloved, Sailed to the West to Mine Gold" (2017 Pushcart Prize nominee)

Poem: "Chea Po Reflects on His Death in Oregon"

Prairie Schooner: "Exile"; "Skull"

Spillway: "What Marjorie Fong Told Caucasians at the Qingming Festival when They Asked if Bodies Came out of the Ground to Eat Food Left for Departed Relatives"

Third Wednesday: "Far from Punyu, Chea Po and Fellow Miners Congregate before the Storm"

Special thanks to Greg Nokes for his book, *Massacred for Gold: The Chinese in Hells Canyon*, which provided the source material from which most of these poems were written.

I am also indebted to Iris Chang's *The Chinese in America* and Arif Dirlik's *Chinese on the American Frontier* for additional inspiration and historical context.

Most importantly, I wish to acknowledge Chea Po and his fellow miners murdered while trying to claim their piece of the American Dream.

Contents

Prologue
Letter from a Chinese Miner in the Snake River
    Country, 1880s   3

Part I *Gum Shan*
Chea Po Sails from China to America,
    Late 19th Century   7
American Dream   8
Chea Po in Lewiston, Idaho, 1883   10
Far from Punyu, Chea Po and Fellow Miners
    Congregate before the Storm   11
Chea Po Remonstrates Ah Yow at Their Gold
    Mining Camp   12
Ah Yow in *Gum Shan*   14
Chea Po to His Diary from Hells Canyon while
    Outlaws Plot His Destruction, 1887   16
The Seasons of Chea Po   18
Exile   19
Meditation on a Chinese Miner   21

Interlude
A Chinese Woman Writes Her Beloved,
    Sailed to the West to Mine Gold   25

Part II Massacre
Chea Po Addresses the Birds Shortly before
    His Murder by Outlaws   29
Chea Po to Himself at Daybreak   30
The Letter Chea Po Never Sends, Spring, 1887   31
Of Miners Murdered in Hells Canyon, May, 1887   32
Chorus   33

Chea Po Reflects on His Death in Oregon 34
Chea Po's Lament 36
Skull 38
Wo Fat, Stranded in the West during the Period
   Known as *The Driving Out*, 1880s 40

Interlude
A Chinese Prostitute in Idaho, Autumn, 1887 45

Part III Trial
Clerk to an Investigative Reporter,
   Wallowa County, Oregon 49
Prospect Park 51
Blue Evans, Fugitive, 1888 53
Question for Frank Vaughan about
   Murdered Chinese Gold Miners 54
James Brewrink's Discovery in Hells Canyon 56
The Code of Wallowa County 58

Interlude
Letter to Chea Po, Butchered for Gold in
   Hells Canyon 61

Part IV Remembering
The Old Chinese Cemetery, Lewiston, Idaho 65
Trip to Chinese Massacre Cove 66
The Door Unhinged 68
Wong Lee Talks Idaho History to a Friend 70
Wong Lee: Memoir Fragment 72
Trial of Compassion, Baker City, Oregon 74
Chinese Remembering Ceremony, 2011 75

Epilogue
What Marjorie Fong Told Caucasians at the
    Qingming Festival when They Asked if Bodies
    Came out of the Ground to Eat Food Left for
    Departed Relatives   79

Glossary   81

About the Author   85

PROLOGUE

Letter from a Chinese Miner in the Snake River Country, 1880s

Wife, the words I write
    from this rough
mining camp are too poor
    an offering for one

who still fires my gnarled, aching body.
    Forgive this fool's gold
an old man sends you. Years
    among barbarians

have stripped from me the hope
    I will feel again
your face between my hands,
    or see our son grow

to marry. Tell me, do you yet
    tend the mulberry trees?
Boil silkworm cocoons to spin
    your delicate threads?

Tonight, at rest by a nameless
    creek, I contemplate
the familiar fields of our village,
    see with the moon's

unerring eye the mat where you sleep.
    Despised by *gweilo*
who once sought our labor,
    we linger like dogs

on the edge of camp, desperate
    for a scrap. Scrape
from stream, from wretched
    gravel a bare, crab-

knuckled existence. Even the air
    we breathe seems metallic.
Each morning when I wake it flares
    my nostrils like the long

cold barrel of a gun. Pray for me,
    wife. Pray to our
Taoist gods that I may prosper
    so you will not starve.

Nor open your door to find
    a friend returned
from *Gum Shan*, my crumbling
    bones his message.

PART I *GUM SHAN*

For increase it is beneficial to cross great rivers.

—The *I Ching*

Chea Po Sails from China to America, Late 19th Century

Suspended. A scavenger on motionless wings.
Caught between the lantern left behind

and the chasm ahead. But memories curled
within like wood shavings remind him

he's made the right choice. The burning temple.
Grain trampled by brigands. And each time

he threw the coins of the *I Ching*
they pointed toward departure.

Unnerving, then, to peer into waves
the day a coastline darkens the horizon

and see a woman's face mouth the question
he can never answer: *How long?*

American Dream

I wonder, Chea Po, how you came to the land
the first immigrants called *Gum Shan*—Gold Mountain.
If you sailed to San Francisco aboard the *Great Republic*,

or perhaps to Portland on the *Belle of Oregon*.
The story of your people in the Northwest,
like the gold you sought at Dead Line Creek,

lies buried under many layers. No one knows
if you, too, left a son behind. If, like thousands,
you laid track for the Northern Pacific Railroad.

Poling a *bateau* into Hells Canyon, your hands
blistered from the ropes when you pulled it
through turbulent water. We know only

that when bodies with bullet holes and limbs
hacked off began to turn up downstream,
they were anonymous. Perhaps Kong Nhan

was among them. Or maybe yours was one
of five skulls found at the massacre site.
Should we be surprised by these bones,

shocked by savagery? No hoe can resist
unbroken earth. Like the Nez Perce,
driven from the Wallowa country ten years

before outlaws descended on your crew like sleet,
you were an exotic rather than a cultivated plant.
A pestilence, an invasive weed to uproot.

What did coins show the last time
you threw them in the temple? In the *I Ching*'s
third hexagram, *Difficulty*, one finds the pitfall

of water above, the movement of thunder below.
And in top yin, a message inscribed like chalk:
Not going forward   Weeping tears of blood

Chea Po in Lewiston, Idaho, 1883

Seeking beneficence, you enter the temple
near mudflats of the Clearwater River.
Though Chinese dug a six-mile ditch

to irrigate the poplars providing shade
for *gweilo*—the Caucasians you call
"white ghosts"—none of these trees

has ever graced your packed streets.
Bowing to the names of five deities,
you light a stick of incense plunged in sand

before you offer liquor to Beuk Aie,
God of the North. A miner, no spirit
means more to you or your fellow

gravel panners than the one who reigns
over the fickle mood of water.
Then you drop the *gau boi*—two rounded

wooden fortune blocks—to consult
your fate. You wonder how long
you will be condemned to remain

in *Gum Shan*, ask if you will ever return
to Guangzhou. They fall flat side up.
A few weeks later, as flames engulf

Chinatown, screaming *gweilo* accost you
in their coarse tongue. Words with challenged
ear you strain to understand: *Let it burn!*

Far from Punyu, Chea Po and Fellow Miners Congregate before the Storm

Last night after we passed the opium pipe
a ragged moon splintered the surface of the creek.
Rocks howled when the river carried Ah Yow away.

It must have been the drug,
because this morning he works beside me.
We smoke to dull the ache from our labor,

but perhaps the gods are sending a message.
Have we been too long in this canyon,
this land itself? Of our women

we hear nothing, and home, our cultured
pearl, seems but a fragment, a fossil
bone that tells a distant story.

This is where the winds have driven us.
First from famine in Guangdong,
then from *gweilo* railroad camps.

Better to sift these waters for gold
than scrub a town's washhouse laundry.
And rumors, gathered like flies to a carcass,

have followed our *bateaus* upriver.
Violence from smoke and gun.
Our shelter reeks of burnt meat,

the spider dangles from its thread.
Why, when I gaze at the night sky,
do the stars tumble from their cage?

Chea Po Remonstrates Ah Yow at Their Gold Mining Camp

For two nights I have barely slept.
Ah Yow keeps farting and cracking jokes.

He raises a terrible stench. One would think
after a long day squatting by the creek

while the sun sears his back, followed
by a sudden chill when it slips

over the canyon rim, he would pass out
on his blanket. How many times I have

wished it were so! But even this petty
request the gods deny. Perhaps they

test me for some greater trial to come.
Last night, when I barked at him in anger,

he merely shrugged and told another joke.
Still, in truth I cannot blame Ah Yow.

I know why his coarse humor rends the night.
Cloud cover obscures the moon, chokes the stars.

In our cramped rock shelter we curl
against each other for warmth.

Such darkness turns one inside out
like a tattered coat, causes even

the strongest to waste away. Ah Yow
had smoked his last opium three days ago.

When a man's life erodes like a river bank
the raven—merciless—lodges in his throat.

Ah Yow in *Gum Shan*

When Chea Po recruited me to mine gold
far up Snake River, I agreed at once.
I wasn't meant to run a washhouse,

and by then most work had disappeared.
I was trapped in an alien land with no means
to return home. Best of all, we would work

for ourselves. No *gweilo* would come with us.
Whispers, vague as summer thunderclouds,
elusive as a swarm of gnats,

scavenge our steps, and from sideways glance
to hard, metallic stare we fence our small garden.
We never know about the *gweilo*. They smile,

then bear down like a flash flood. When we
built their railroads, though life was hard,
we at least had work. But then a bleak rain

that melted the jobs away began to fall.
Now I have been many months with Chea Po.
To keep spirits up I gamble and tell jokes.

Sometimes my only recourse is the opium pipe.
We don't speak about what the wind
may bring, the bird that haunts my shoulder.

Only of our return across the sea.
With gold we may at last leave *Gum Shan*,
the men with guns on their hips.

But two nights ago the moon
seared my callused palm. I felt pinned
by a pair of talons. Dreamed I'd lost my head.

Chea Po to His Diary from Hells Canyon while Outlaws Plot His Destruction, 1887

Late spring. We are nearing now the end
   of our venture on waters the *gweilo*
call Snake River and Dead Line Creek.
   We have sifted much gold with our pans.
Kong Nhan and Chea Sun talk every day
   about their return to China before the winter
snows. I smile—a mask—but a dark shape
   troubles my mind. Here in this great
canyon south of the *gweilo's* Lewiston we are
   cut off from the world. Strangers trying
to survive a hostile land. We see no one,
   yet talons of the silent-winged owl
constrict my breath. Last month, my blood
   in turmoil, I consulted the *I Ching*. I tossed
the coins a short distance from the crew.
   Orion the hunter lit the sky above. The
hexagram showed by the coins was number 21,
   Shih Ho, which means "biting through."

Above Li   The Clinging, Fire
Below Chện   The Arousing, Thunder

An obstruction has manifested. I ponder what
   this could mean. Perhaps our return home?
If so, who or what would obstruct us? A week ago
   I again consulted the oracle. This time the coins
pointed to *Po*, hexagram 23. Splitting apart.
   Six in the second place means the power
of the negative forces around us grows stronger.
   Again, I do not see clearly what this could
mean. Each morning we awaken to river and cliffs.

   To birds and at times a lone wild sheep.
Yet the signs grow ever more opposed. Last night
   I threw the coins once more. Now I am
truly fearful. For I drew the 29th hexagram:
   K'an, the Abysmal (Water). The doubling
of the trigram signals great danger. Worse, six
   at the top means my own irresponsible
actions have brought this danger upon myself
   and my men. Have I indeed put pride
and greed above our welfare? Gone astray
   from the Tao? All my life I have obeyed
its supple flow. Yet now the path to the creek
   feels cursed, a cloud into which I vanish.

The Seasons of Chea Po

Springtime crane in the grain field.

Summer flight above the temple.

Autumn migration.

Winter feathers on the river.

Exile

No tool in your miner's arsenal, Chea Po,
no toss of the *I Ching's* coins,
could divine the depths of separation.
Stretch out your arm, flick the coal

from a twist of burning tobacco,
and neither movement describes it.
Only feeling gives a clue, and even that
is crude, inexact—a mockery of measure.

When you left for the American West
did you have a timeline, a plan?
Or did you flee bandits and famine
only to watch a black moon betray you?

In either case, the sum of the equation
remains the same. A secret weight,
heavier on the scales than any gold
you may have found in Hells Canyon.

You must have envied the eagle aloft
on thermal currents, the sure-footed
bighorn sheep who climbed those walls.
Able to do what you could not. So at home,

so integrated into their surroundings it took
a trained eye to spot them. Not like you
and the other Chinese who fled Lewiston
last fall to cast your fates upriver.

Always deer in the gun-sights, you now
roam the gravel bar of Deep Creek
with your placer pan, more isolated,
it would seem, than even those animals

whose freedom you would emulate.
Unaware, as the sounds of water
intertwine themselves in your dark ache,
of rifles riding down to destroy it.

Meditation on a Chinese Miner

*Let's do our country a favor and kill off the Chinese
and get the gold for our trouble.*
      —gang member, Wallowa County, Oregon

Morning sun burnishes the upper cliffs.
Such color drives your search.
But when you emerge
from your rock shelter to relieve yourself
a bitter wind
scours the canyon's depths.

Last night you ate dried bamboo
with your rice. Smoked opium to dull

                    your aching back.

For months you've courted an eagle above the rim.
A jade-flecked dream dangles from its beak.
Yours takes you back to Guangzhou.
Years in the American West have sucked
its moisture away, much as a young wasp
consumes its caterpillar host from within.

By now it's become brittle and sere.
This life reduced to heat and cold,
labor and solitude
has become for you a home.
An accretion like mineral build-up,
a shell clamped around a crab.

Cliffs tumbling to the cove, lanterns
spreading their glow along the gravel bar—
if these parallel the calm

ordained by your Taoist heart
are you renewed by your crippling toil?
Will it reconcile you when you turn to face,

boiling out from multiple ambush sites,
a sudden squall, a dark shower of lead?

INTERLUDE

A Chinese Woman Writes Her Beloved, Sailed to the West to Mine Gold

Of the years you have been gone, my husband,
    only the crane on its migration keeps count.
This loneliness, more barren than my womb,
    brands my skin, leaches what remains of its luster.

For months after you took ship I made visits
    to the temple. I sounded the gong
to announce my presence, lit incense,
    bowed before the *chin-hua*, the sacred bouquets.

Some days I shook a fortune stick from its case.
    Others, I offered liquor to the spirits. I prayed
to Beuk Aie, the God of Water, to favor you.
    To Toy Guon, the God of Riches, to reward

your efforts so you might return. To Guan Yin,
    the Goddess of Mercy, to show compassion.
I swore when they would not answer,
    wished I had never bound myself

to a Gold Mountain man. Neither ginseng
    nor burdock root bring me relief. Famine
and bandits ravage our village, and word
    from you withers like a severed limb.

Who can tell me the disposition of the waters?
    Whether their music soothes your sleep?
Or floods a gravel bar with bones from which
    the moon draws forth a wild mineral gleam?

PART II MASSACRE

*There is nothing that can be said in favor of the Chinese.
We must get rid of them.*

—Judge A. Heed, Ogden, Utah, 1885

Chea Po Addresses the Birds Shortly before His Murder by Outlaws

For many months I have toiled in the wilderness,
and the years in *Gum Shan*, this strange country
the *gweilo* named *America*, blur like bamboo.

Each day on the canyon floor begins in shadow.
When the upper cliffs glow like brass,
I scurry under an umbrella of spilled ink.

Panning for gold, I hear the river muffle
a strangled voice, lament our women
left behind in China.

And you, o birds, how you mock us
with your wings, your song!
Lighter than air, you flit from branch

to branch held aloft by feathers,
by hollow bones. The hungry hawk
burns my face with longing.

At night I trace Orion's journey.
For a brief time it stalks the dark walls.
Then, like the flash of a muzzle, snuffs out.

Chea Po to Himself at Daybreak

Breath. My spirit. An exiled crane
the cold displays abandoned by the moon.

Far above, dawn splashes the basaltic rim.
I dream of simple pleasures: a bowl

of steamed noodles in Guangzhou. The click
of many chopsticks when rain gutters the road.

Each day for months now like the last:
this water freezing my hands

as I sift sand and gravel for gold,
the river's thunder

a troubling rumble within the temple.
I who have always known the names

of things—this tree or that stone,
the strange four-legged creature

scampering among the rocks—have become
a straw man. Unable to speak the future.

Breath, you evaporate while I shiver.
Vacate this crabbed husk.

Afraid of the yellow bolt
that comes to steal the living.

The Letter Chea Po Never Sends, Spring, 1887

Too long have I risen in darkness among rough men
hawking and spitting, rubbing together chapped hands
to ward off the cold. Too distant now the elegant
crane draped in folds of light.
Do you remember, wife,
how we marveled at their flight the evening I proposed?
A sign of good luck, we agreed.
Yet here at the bottom of a canyon in *Gum Shan*,
not all the gold flakes we have panned
from its waters seem worth the bargain.
Too late I have learned my true fortune
lay in your whisper, the rustle your garments
made as you crossed the floor. And when I scan
the sky I see not the winged smoke
we so admired, but predators sustained by updraft
always circling, as if they know something
of which we remain unaware. A future
even the gods withhold,
as the ocean keeps from me the treasure of your breast.
Each day I take less pleasure in the sound
of men's voices, the profane oaths not meant
for your ear. Hemmed in by current and cliff,
I long for a path, a sign. A giving way.

Of Miners Murdered in Hells Canyon, May, 1887

The first body, found at Lime Kiln,
betrayed a bullet hole
below the right shoulder blade.
Two cuts from an axe scarred the head.

The second, recovered at Penewawa Bar
a hundred miles north of the massacre site,
had been shot near the heart,
its head severely chopped.

The third, Chea Po, was your companion Ah Yow,
fished from a drift pile at Log Cabin Bar.
He'd been shot twice in the back.
The severed head, along with his left arm,
was strapped to the corpse with his belt.

That fall a rancher stumbled upon skeletons
deep in the canyon. They'd washed up
on gravel or come to rest in the rocks.
Because coyotes and buzzards
had stripped them clean,
he couldn't tell they were Chinese.

Neither could the river.
Indifferent, it gathered all
who swirled within its grasp.
Whether it carried silt, branch or bone
mattered only to those who came later,

who fleshed a history from the wreckage.

Chorus

We are the blood, the nectar,
voices of the many that speak as one.

The hatchling, the flight of the migratory
flock—these we prepare, we own.

From conception we nourished Chea Po.
Directed his first clumsy steps.

When with fever he clutched his wife,
we flooded his member to propel him

between her hips. Those still mornings
he watched her sweep the floor clean

or boil water for tea, steam rising
like laughter, we formed a great pool.

Now, delivered from creek, from canyon
hiding its gold far from his home country,

he lies broken on a gravel bar.
Bullets and a hatchet's spare glint

free us to pollute the water, to stain the sand.
Drained of power, we suffer the earth's

rebuke, the scorn of a river that murmurs
among the rocks, *Unclean! Unclean!*

Chea Po Reflects on His Death in Oregon

When the bullets struck, my body pitched
    to the ground. Even before
it hit I was drifting somewhere above.
    I saw the bodies of friends

hacked and thrown in the river.
    Whether mine
was among them or remained
    on the gravel bar

is unclear. But I cannot erase the sight
    of a man beheading Ah Yow
as he grabbed the gold, our gear gone
    to flame. The night before

I had thrown a bowl of rice at him
    for loosing much wind
in our cramped shelter as we ate.
    But he ducked,

the bowl shattered against the rock wall
    and showered him
with hot grain. Ah Yow was always
    joking to ease the weight

of our labor. Panning for gold
    we either baked
or froze—not much in between.
    Like me, he had been

many years in this blunt, uncultured land.
    What I would give,
he told me, *to walk again across*
    a curved dragon bridge,

to see moon gates, a teahouse bathed in mist!
    Now a black-winged cloud
drips blood. How can it fulfill its duty?
    Shroud a nesting crane?

Chea Po's Lament

Since that day we were ambushed
    and butchered
in the canyon I have wandered,
    disembodied,

over *Gum Shan*. Condemned to do so
    forever because no one
tends our graves. And I can see now
    it wasn't

just our gold the *gweilo* gunmen wanted.
    We would
have given it gladly to save our lives.
    Rather, it was *us*

with rifles and hatchets they came for.
    Hating the long queues
dangling to our waists, the conical bamboo
    hats, the strange sing-song

tongue that drifted above the river.
    And what did
our yellow skin seem to them
    but fool's gold?

We who were already old, inventors
    of silk, paper, porcelain,
the gunpowder they used to pour into us
    their lethal fire.

To be killed by one of our own in China—
    that I could accept—
but to be denied a peaceful resting place by *gweilo*...
    there are no words.

Each day I miss Ah Yow's silly jokes,
    the music of the waters.
Do not speak to me of the gods to whom
    we burned joss sticks

in the temple. They have abandoned us.
    Violence, drought,
the bitter cold of a *Gum Shan* winter—
    all have obscured them.

From this point forward let no man praise
    the sun, the moon's pale dress.
Nor claim he knows the Tao. Which way
    it bends or how far.

Skull

Long after the flesh had vanished
a sheepherder found it at Deep Creek.

It belonged to one of the Chinese miners
massacred for gold in Hells Canyon.

A bullet had blown a whole section
away, but this did not discourage

the sheepherder from turning it
into a sugar bowl. The sort

of relic one might find
in a collectibles store or the dusty,

web-framed attic of an eccentric
who died of cumulative failure.

Was it you, Chea Po, who contained
this sweetness? Held its promise?

I like to think you weren't one
of the bodies washed up downstream

after weeks in the river.
That you remained on a gravel bar

where you'd panned for flakes,
watched by wary bighorns. It is important

for me—a stranger writing over a century
after the murders—to imagine you there.

More than artifact the morning light reveals.
For whom water speaks a lost language.

Wo Fat, Stranded in the West during the Period Known as *The Driving Out*, 1880s

You ask about the miners murdered last year
in Hells Canyon. I knew Chea Po.
Gambled and smoked opium with his crew.
We came from the same small town in China.
During times of hunger I saw women so desperate
they ate clay and men who chewed bark from trees.
A peasant could never tell when bandits might storm

his village. One day crimps shanghaied a distant
cousin for what you *lo fang* call the "coolie" trade.
They held him in a *zhuzi guan*—a filthy barracoon.
Chained to a rotting corpse before they shipped him,
still shackled, to a Cuban sugar plantation. The Chinese
there had to work twenty-one hours a day on "meals"
of three unripe bananas. Did you know that?

We never saw him again.

I have spent over half my life in *Gum Shan*.
When I labored on your railroad
winter snows reached drifts of eighty feet.
Wang Lee and Ah Ho disappeared in a blizzard.
After the spring melt we found them still upright,
frozen to their shovels. Chow Yun, my sister's
husband, dropped a vial of nitroglycerin.
I lost friends to landslides,
the fickle winds of *lo fang* violence.

I never hear from my family. Years ago I stopped
sending money. Perhaps they no longer live.

For a time I had a new wife in Idaho.
But a customer killed her
when she demanded he pay for her bed.

From my boxcar, abandoned by the railroad,
spirits whisper when clouds
betray the moon:

This place is now your home.

INTERLUDE

A Chinese Prostitute in Idaho, Autumn, 1887

I am a lotus blossom claimed by Gold Mountain,
by this dark siren *Gum Shan*. Men who control
the opium trade bought me from my parents.

Our village is poor and my father gambles too much.
The youngest daughter is ever at risk. He sold me
as a *mui tsai*, a "little sister." One who works

for a family, then marries at eighteen. Ah, the artful
treachery of language! After I crossed the ocean,
a trip of two months beset by scurvy, stench,

the many corpses thrown overboard, I became
a *loungei*, a woman who always holds up her legs.
For three years I've entertained men starved

for pleasure. At least fortune favors me more
than Mai-ling, branded on the shoulder
because she dared to leave her crib.

Three years. Yet how unkind the mirror!
My breasts, my damp tunnel, ache with rough secrets.
People ask if I knew Chea Po, one of the miners

murdered last spring in Hells Canyon. I cannot say
for certain. Many men come to our door.
Whatever riches they plumb between my thighs,

they themselves remain shadows on the wall.
I do what I must. Opium helps me endure.
It is easy to come by, and a smoke takes me

far from my cares, from *America*.
As for that unlucky man and those others
killed with him, I light incense in their memory.

I petition the gods to bless them with a soft rain,
to watch over them in the spirit world.
I no longer pray for deliverance.

PART III TRIAL

I guess if they had killed thirty-one white men something would have been done about it, but none of the jury knew the Chinese or cared much about it, so they turned the men loose.

—George Craig, rancher, Wallowa County, Oregon, about the May 25, 1887 massacre of over thirty Chinese gold miners in Hells Canyon, and subsequent trial.

Clerk to an Investigative Reporter, Wallowa County, Oregon

You don't ask and you don't tell.
—Judge Ben Boswell

Well, yes, I hid the trial records of the massacre.
I did it to protect the interests of the county.
Some of the killers have family here,

people I've known all my life.
They're good folks, just like the pioneers
who settled this valley. They built communities

and worked the land.
Before them it was just Indians.
I mean, they never *improved* anything.

Sooner or later they were going to have to go.
And as for those Chinese miners down on
Deep Creek, it's terrible they were slaughtered

like that, but I've always wanted to showcase
the positives about the county. It's not fair
to have one incident define who we are.

I know you're shocked that we include
the gang leader with those people
who first civilized this area,

but he helped build the county, too.
Anyway, that was such a long time ago.
People have forgotten about it

or never much cared in the first place.
It's kind of lost to history now. Why dig it up
and ruffle feathers? I'm proud I served forty-five

years in this office. If you really want to see what
we're all about, come to Chief Joseph Days.
We celebrate our heritage.

Prospect Park

Of the bodies, Chea Po, we know only fragments.
Some, thrown into the river by the killers,
floated downstream to Lewiston. If this indeed
is where you lie, people who picnic
above you have found what the Chinese
wished it to remain when they sold it:

a pleasant place. The view of the Clearwater
pouring into the Snake,
of grasses glazing the far side like lacquer,
a fine enamel, is one you knew by heart.
How many times,
watching a fiery ball scorch the horizon,

must you have felt it burn
a path across the sea to Guangzhou?
Chinese who stepped down the gangplank
bearing bamboo poles over their shoulders
bore another weight: buried untended here,
they would always be forced to wander.

You have invaded my senses,
not as a body shot and cleaved with an axe,
but a spirit aggrieved.
Now unearthed, fluid as the creek you panned.
The gods you invoked with incense
and liquor, with fervent

supplication, failed to protect
your crew from a murderous gang.
Or the temple, itself but a memory.

In the West, even deities have learned
that to survive
it is sometimes best to go armed.

Blue Evans, Fugitive, 1888

My gang murdered the Chinese miners
down on Snake River last year.
Tongues of fire, that's what we were.
Black-shrouded scythes of death.
Each time our rifles spat,
the smell of powder goaded
the ripe trigger finger.
Those the bullets didn't kill,
our hatchets, raised high
in the hot-blooded air,
sent to perdition, to night.

Because the truth is those damn Orientals
don't belong in white man's country.
We took their gold, all right,
but no pigtailed heathen
who speaks that jargon
they call a language
could ever be one of us.
Not now, not ever.
Eleven years ago
we drove the Nez Perce out.
Now it's the Chinaman's turn.

This is America. The eagle
riding a cold, bitter wind.

Question for Frank Vaughan about Murdered Chinese Gold Miners

In this grainy photo from the early 20th century
    West we see, along with a mop slanted
against a cabin of unfinished lumber

and white caulking, four men,
    three of them old and weathered.
Behind them stand their wives, women

of undetermined middle age, hair drawn tightly
    up and back, faces severe beneath their shawls.
Over your shoulder your small boy hints at a smile,

but he's more bemused, the mouth curled at the corners
    with a shy, incipient pucker, as if rolling his tongue
over a piece of sour hard candy.

A group that evokes the thorny word, *clan*.
    One thinks of Jesse James, the friends
and kinfolk who shielded him

in Clay County, Missouri. But this is Oregon
    some thirty years and a lot of dead
outlaws later. And you, Frank,

glaring into the camera
    with your droopy mustache,
blacksmith tongs gripped in the left hand

while you stroke a dog with the other,
    hold the viewer hostage. Unable to let go.
The observer who somehow fathoms

beneath the goatee, the sunken eyes
    and rough homestead charm,
those rustling secrets buried and left

behind when you decided to go straight.
    Or is it a bloody moon you deny?
Its dense, clotting rain?

James Brewrink's Discovery in Hells Canyon

Only six in 1910, you descend
to a gravel bar on the river.

You're not prepared
for screams suspended

above five gaping skulls
you locate among the rocks,

their story fled from onion eyes.
From sockets obscene without flesh

to brittle, smoke-stained teeth,
you scan a harsh script.

These relics,
along with other remains

strewn across the narrow bar,
have weathered here over twenty years.

You know none of this. Your family
never speaks of the Chinese miners

slaughtered by Blue Evans' gang.
That's a bruise they hide.

The canyon grows thistles and snakes,
its river a runaway train.

Such land is more than enough
to hold you. But the moment you see

the skulls you tell yourself
bones raked by wind harbor secrets.

What language, what silent syllables,
do these fragments speak even now?

Walled off by age, by horror,
it's beyond you to translate such a text.

While your father begins to hack
the stony ground with whatever

makeshift tools he has, you're startled
to hear cut through the river's

roar your own shrill voice:
Fill in the holes!

The Code of Wallowa County

> *There are some really weird feelings in this county.*
> —Bruce Womack, former Forest Service archaeologist

Your killers were never punished, Chea Po.
Of the men who massacred you

and your fellow miners, three were found
not guilty and the rest fled the scene.

Silenced by family and friends, your story
decomposed faster than the bodies

flushed from Hells Canyon by the river.
And what can one say about the memorial

arch the people of Enterprise put up
to commemorate the valley's pioneers?

Whatever notion of justice you may
have harbored for your companions

when furies no opium stupor could conjure
unleashed themselves to gun you down,

then mutilate with blades of whetted steel,
consider that the name of the gang's leader

adorns the arch's left column. If you
could look through it you would see,

framed within that confining brick,
the Wallowa County Courthouse.

INTERLUDE

Letter to Chea Po, Butchered for Gold in Hells Canyon

From the kitchen window I savor
    a dense wall of bamboo.
The drooped shape
    of its narrow, pointed
leaves evokes a protective shower,
    a feathery cloak
deflecting a barrage of hail.
    The seasons of the natural world,
their speckled rhythms,
    never fail to instruct.

I cannot contemplate these stalks
    and fail to conjure you,
Chea, shot so long ago when lead
    flared down from a sky
already burning with menace.
    Just now a junco
landed on a feeder
    hanging from a potted plant.
These images, like the snow's
    mute blade,
arise to salt a wound. How is it
    possible this lesion,
like the fracture of the canyon
    itself, can span
time's gorge? Draw a thin
    streak of blood
for someone I never knew?
    If I could appear
along Deep Creek before
    the firestorm

broke from the canyon's walls
    would I,
armed with foreknowledge,
    be able
to convince you to cut loose
    your *bateau* and flee?
Would my awkward gesture
    make a difference?

You knew that bamboo displays
    healthy leaves
with those about to die.
    This moment
it's these soft wet flakes
    blanketing
shrub and field. How they
    spur,
after a long suspended breath,
    a resurrection.

PART IV REMEMBERING

My grandfather came to this country from China nearly a century ago and worked as a servant. Now I serve as governor just one mile from where my grandfather worked. It took our family one hundred years to travel that mile. It was a voyage we could only make in America.

—Governor Gary Locke of Washington state,
the first Chinese-American governor in
the United States, January 28, 2003

The Old Chinese Cemetery, Lewiston, Idaho

Do I walk above your bones, Chea Po?
Or those of Chea Sun, whose battered pan,
like yours, sifted sand and gravel from frigid
Northwest streams? Each step shakes
dead leaves from their own wet grave.

We'll never know where you lie.
Maybe here. Maybe in Hells Canyon.
Or did you, a mere trace mineral, drift far
beyond this town, carrion for coyote and crow?

You didn't see these trim houses
line the opposite bluff, nor industrial blight
below what long has been a park.
But spines of earth
plunging like collapsed bridges to the confluence

of the Snake and Clearwater rivers
mirror a vision, the one your eye
melded to a dream inhaled like opium:
gold was your only ticket home.

Across the street, two pumpkins guard the entry
to a porch. Ribbons of dried corn leaves
scrolled up its columns mock the treasure
you sought along Deep Creek the day horse thieves
destroyed your crew with rifle, hatchet, stone.

Because you hoarded shiny flakes.
Because a raven darkened their gun sights.
Because no one would convict.
Because a man can pop lice with his teeth.

Trip to Chinese Massacre Cove

Early summer snowmelt roils the Snake River,
    brings branches, logs, that seemingly innocent
        stick the jet boat swerves to avoid.

Suck it in and the engine rasps like a logger
    ravaged by nicotine, a husk
        who can no longer wield a chainsaw.

What, then, would we think to see bodies
    impossible to name borne on this current?
        So burdened by death, a hatchet's

grim work, as to strangle the loosest tongue.
    Where you poled and portaged *bateaus*,
        Chea Po, we power upstream with nothing

but a mishandled camera, an ill-fitting hat,
    to lose. A cold, wet spring has nourished
        Hells Canyon. Blind to history,

bighorn sheep cling to the rocky heights.
    Three miles from the cove
        a still visible track scars the canyon wall.

The route taken by Nez Perce driven from their
    Wallowa homeland. They survived
        where you did not. As you struggled

to ascend rapids like Wild Goose, did you notice
    great blue herons on the Idaho side?
        They would have ignored the bodies

the current swept past them. Even alive the Chinese
    were but curiosa: weird, alien, outlandish.
        In present day Lewiston they have become

relics boxed up and stored under glass.
    Drenched by a rapid's violent spray,
        we splutter as a heron spears his lunch.

The Door Unhinged

Where you knew community, Chea Po, only a solitary
    marker reminds us
how your people came, settled, then dispersed
    like milkweed
when work dried up. Fugitive ghosts drift
    above the Clearwater River,
their memory long since paved over. When you left
    in '86 for Hells Canyon,
had the banshee wind that destroyed so many Chinese
    the year before
already reached your ear? Poured through broken
    windows, torn laundry from the line?

Once welcomed as dynamiters, as cheap coolie labor,
    now bludgeoned, shot,
burned alive. Surely you'd heard:
    three hundred
dumped in the rain-soaked winter forest
    outside Tacoma,
their homes sacked, then put to the torch.
    The baleful
ascent of the raptor, the Hun salting the land
    with skulls.

Did you query the moon, ask why she withdrew
    her glow
and fled behind the clouds? Or cast
    with dark eyes
the tantalizing coins, strain to divine
    a comet in the night?
You would become another of these statistics,
    you and others

who poled their *bateaus* upriver to sift creeks
    for flour gold.
No return to your fraternal club, the Hip Sing Tong,
    nor liquor
offered to Beuk Aie, the water god who denied
    your prayers.

Even as bullets and axes dismembered your companions
    the Tao,
like an old threadbare carpet, had unraveled
    at the edges.
People already were beginning to move away.
    Permanence,
you understood, is illusion. This afternoon a cow
    elk wanders
grassland atop the bluff. Breathes the alarm
    of approaching winter.

Wong Lee Talks Idaho History to a Friend

This photo here? That's my grandfather, Wong Shu.
    He came to America in 1881, a year before Congress
        passed the Chinese Exclusion Act. When he walked
down the gangplank he looked like any other villager

from Guangdong: loose-fitting blue cotton blouse, baggy
    breeches, split bamboo hat, hair plaited in a queue.
        His belongings hung from both ends of a pole
borne upon his shoulders. But over time that changed.

Long odds on the frontier sowed the devil in him.
    Notice the revolver and gun belt, the bowie knife
        on the opposite hip. It didn't matter who you were,
Chinese or white. Cross him and you'd bleed.

He planned to join Chea Po's gold mining crew,
    the one murdered by outlaws in Hells Canyon.
        But he was stabbed in a knife fight before they left
town. It took two months to recover. Meanwhile,

decomposed bodies began to fetch up on rocks and gravel
    bars along the Snake. It was a bad omen. When he
        regained his health he drifted down to the Boise Basin.
That's where this picture was taken.

As you know, it was custom to marry and father a child
    before leaving home. The man had more reason to return.
        Wong Shu indeed had done so while in China.
But years of struggle dimmed his memory.

Like many Chinese, he loved to gamble.
    He married a prostitute he won in a card game.
        That's my grandmother in this other photograph.
Although she was still young, circumstances had laid

their brand on her. They died when I was just a boy.
    Sometimes they brought me small cakes.
        But if I asked about their lives in the West
only their eyes gave voice, flushed like startled geese.

Wong Lee: Memoir Fragment

My father remembers flying kites in Idaho City as a boy,
  firecrackers during Chinese New Year, elaborate

funeral processions. All gone now. It's become
  a ghost town. Chinese there a century ago

held their own. Some went well-armed. Unlike Chea Po's
  doomed gold seekers, we suffered no massacre.

But when mining played out, we and the whites both left.
  Our family moved to Portland, where they prospered

as merchants. My father inherited a dry goods store,
  but I got a scholarship to Berkeley. As an engineer

I live well. I have a house in the hills. Today, however,
  a white neighbor asked my son whose side he would

take in a war with China. I sighed when he told me this.
  How does he make the man see the washed out road,

the cliffs with no guardrail around a curve? We are now
  four generations in this country. My son speaks English

better than Chinese. He has no desire to visit China.
  Too crowded, he says. Too rigid. My grandfather

prayed to the water god in a joss house. My father
  became a Christian. Though I have no gods, the same

cannot be said of my son. He needs no incense, no carved nor graven image to worship Michael Jordan.

Trial of Compassion, Baker City, Oregon

Most of them wanted to return to China.
That's all they thought about.
                              —Marjorie Fong

What she sees with eyes undaunted
    by age will never rival
the memory she summons like a falconer.
    When that bird arrives, given

ferocious wing, it gifts her vision
    so that it blinds,
a picture imprinted like a bed of nails.
    Today her wheelchaired

body trembles when she recalls the thugs
    who dragged a wooden Buddha
from the temple and chopped it to pieces.
    Just a child then, her parents merchants

in the town when Chinese laundered, mined,
    sold vegetables they grew. Now
a footnote to history, the temple demolished
    to make way for an office building.

Unfathomable, those *gweilo*! Who would be
    so rude, so dull, to profane a carving?
Gone rigid, she clamps hard on the wheels.
    Watches yet again the serene face

fly apart cocooned by laughter. Traces
    through brilliance the swift downward
arc of steel, chilled—as splinters blight
    the street—by a wounding rain.

Chinese Remembering Ceremony, 2011

I walk the same burr-infested ground
you and other miners knew,
Chea Po, the ground your blood defiled.

We should all die in such a place.

The trail to the low rock shelter
winds through wild aster, Queen Anne's lace,
the rich, buttery blossoms of prickly pear cactus.
Rain-greened cliffs amplify the river below.
Arrived during a more settled time,
we can afford to linger over such details.

This June the Snake, bloated with snowmelt,
covers the gravel bar where you died.
Only a tiny ribbon of sand lies exposed.
A few butterflies, black with gold borders,
have alighted there. The colors of death
and the dream you pursued to the end.

At the ruins of your shelter a small
monument honors the dead. A Nez Perce
and two Chinese have come with us
to the massacre site. Whites comprise the rest.
Those for whom atonement is itself an ore,
one whose value climbs on the thermals.

A man points to steep terrain north and south.
Here gang members set up their ambush.
Silence wraps like a towel around the invocation.

A gong brought all the way from Lewiston,
struck for each of the murdered miners,
reverberates among the cliffs.

One by one we grasp burning sticks of incense
and bow three times.

Holding the paper likeness
of an ingot, I thrust it into flame.

Nothing speaks but water.

EPILOGUE

What Marjorie Fong Told Caucasians at the Qingming
Festival when They Asked if Bodies Came out of the
Ground to Eat Food Left for Departed Relatives

Do your people come up and smell the flowers?

Glossary

barracoon   A place of temporary confinement for slaves or convicts.

bateau   French for a double-ended flat-bottomed rowboat used on rivers in Canada and some parts of the U.S.

Cantonese   Dialect spoken in southeast China and Hong Kong.

Chief Joseph Days   An annual festival and rodeo held each summer in Joseph, Oregon. Named for Chief Joseph of the Nez Perce, who led bands of those Indians in their fateful war against the U.S. Government in 1877.

chin-hua   Sacred bouquets placed before an altar in a Taoist temple.

crib   A tiny shack no larger than twelve by fourteen feet facing a narrow alley that served as a low-class brothel for Chinese women sold or forced into prostitution in the 19th century American West..

crimp   An unscrupulous Chinese recruiter in the business of replacing African slave labor with Asian slave labor on colonial plantations in the Caribbean and South America.

Dead Line Creek   A small creek that flows into the Snake River on the Oregon side of Hells Canyon. Later renamed Deep Creek, it was at its convergence with the Snake that Chea Po and his fellow miners were murdered on May 25, 1887.

gau-boi   Rounded wooden fortune blocks.

Guangdong The southeast province that sent the majority of 19th century Chinese immigrants to America.

Guangzhou Port city in the Chinese province of Guangdong.

Gum Shan Literally meaning "Gold Mountain," this was the term used to designate America by 19th century Chinese who immigrated there. As for generations of Europeans, Chinese faced with starvation, banditry, political upheaval and violence at home viewed America as a land of opportunity.

gweilo A Cantonese word for Caucasians meaning "white ghost."

I Ching Considered the oldest of the Chinese classics, the I Ching, or Book of Changes, is an oracular document of fundamental principles represented by 64 hexagrams. Their positions were associated with varying conditions and predictions for improvement and avoidance of danger.

joss A Chinese idol.

joss house A Chinese temple.

lo fang Another Cantonese expression for "Caucasian."

loungei Cantonese for "prostitute."

mui tsai A Cantonese term meaning "little sister," which referred to a girl sold to a family who worked for it until she was eighteen and then married.

Nez Perce A Northwest Plateau Indian tribe whose traditional homeland comprised parts of Oregon, Washington and Idaho.

Orion   A giant-sized hunter in Classical mythology, Orion, with his three-starred "belt," is one of the most visible and best known constellations in the night sky.

Punyu   A district of the port city of Guangzhou.

Qingming Festival   A Chinese celebration of ancestors and departed loved ones.

tael   A former Chinese money of account, being the value of this weight of standard silver. From the Malay word *tahil*.

Tao   Literally, "The Way." Taoism, the religion of the majority of 19th century Chinese laborers who came to America, was a system developed by Lao-tzu and Chung-tzu advocating a life of complete simplicity and naturalness, and of non-interference with the course of natural events in order to attain a happy existence in harmony with the Tao.

Wallowa   The name of a county in northeast Oregon, as well as a lake, river, valley and mountains it contains. The Wallowa Valley was the traditional homeland of many Nez Perce Indians until their eviction in 1877 by the U.S. Government. The word means "winding water" in the Nez Perce language.

yin   In Chinese religion and philosophy, a negative principle, dark and feminine, in contrast to the positive principle, bright and masculine, of *yang*. Their interaction is supposed to influence the destinies of creatures and things.

zhuzi guan   Literally meaning "pig pens," this is the Chinese expression for "barracoon."

About the Author

Peter Ludwin is the recipient of a Literary Fellowship from Artist Trust and the W.D. Snodgrass Award for Endeavor and Excellence in Poetry. His first book, *A Guest in All Your Houses*, was published in 2009 by Word Walker Press. His second collection is *Rumors of Fallible Gods*, a two-time finalist for the Gival Press Poetry Award that was published in 2013 by Presa Press.

Gone to Gold Mountain in its original smaller chapbook form was a semi-finalist for both the 2010 Concrete Wolf Chapbook Award and the Floating Bridge Press Chapbook Award.

Ludwin was the Second Prize Winner of the 2007-2008 Anna Davidson Rosenberg Awards, and a finalist during the same period for *The Comstock Review's* Muriel Craft Bailey Memorial Award. In 2010 he was nominated for a Pushcart Prize. The following year he received Special Merit Recognition from *The Comstock Review*, and *Soundings Review* named him its Readers' Choice winner in the spring/summer issue.

A finalist in poetry for the 2016 Tucson Festival of Books Literary Awards, as well as the Second Place poetry winner in the 2016 Kay Snow Writing Awards sponsored by Willamette Writers, Ludwin was the 2016 winner of the Muriel Craft Bailey Memorial Award. From 2002-2013 he was a participant in the San Miguel Poetry Week in San Miguel de Allende, Mexico, where he workshopped under noted poets such as Mark Doty, Forrest Gander, Tony Hoagland, Joseph Stroud and Robert Wrigley.

His work has appeared in many journals, including *Atlanta Review*, *The Bitter Oleander*, *The Comstock Review*, *Crab Orchard Review*, *Nimrod*, *North American Review* and *Prairie Schooner*.

Ludwin considers himself a firm advocate of Scottish poet Alastair Reid's dictum, "Listen to how it sounds on the ear," and names as significant influences the language he encountered in *The Adventures of Robin Hood* as a boy, Rainer Maria Rilke's *New Poems*, Theodore Roethke, Dylan Thomas, James Dickey, James Wright, Federico García Lorca, Pablo Neruda and, among contemporary poets, Mark Doty, Joseph Fasano, Pattiann Rogers, Joseph Stroud and Robert Wrigley. Other major influences include the natural world, foreign cultures and music—he plays acoustic blues guitar and traditional American and Celtic tunes on the autoharp, and has both performed and taught at the Pacific Northwest Folklife Festival.

An avid traveler who has journeyed by canoe to visit remote Indian families in the Amazon Basin of Ecuador, hiked in the Peruvian Andes, thumbed for rides in Greece and bargained for goods in the markets of Marrakech and Istanbul, he endured a debilitating illness for three weeks in 2011 while visiting China and Tibet.

He lives in Kent, Washington, where he works for the Parks Department.

www.ingramcontent.com/pod-product-compliance
Lightning Source LLC
Chambersburg PA
CBHW021156080526
44588CB00008B/368